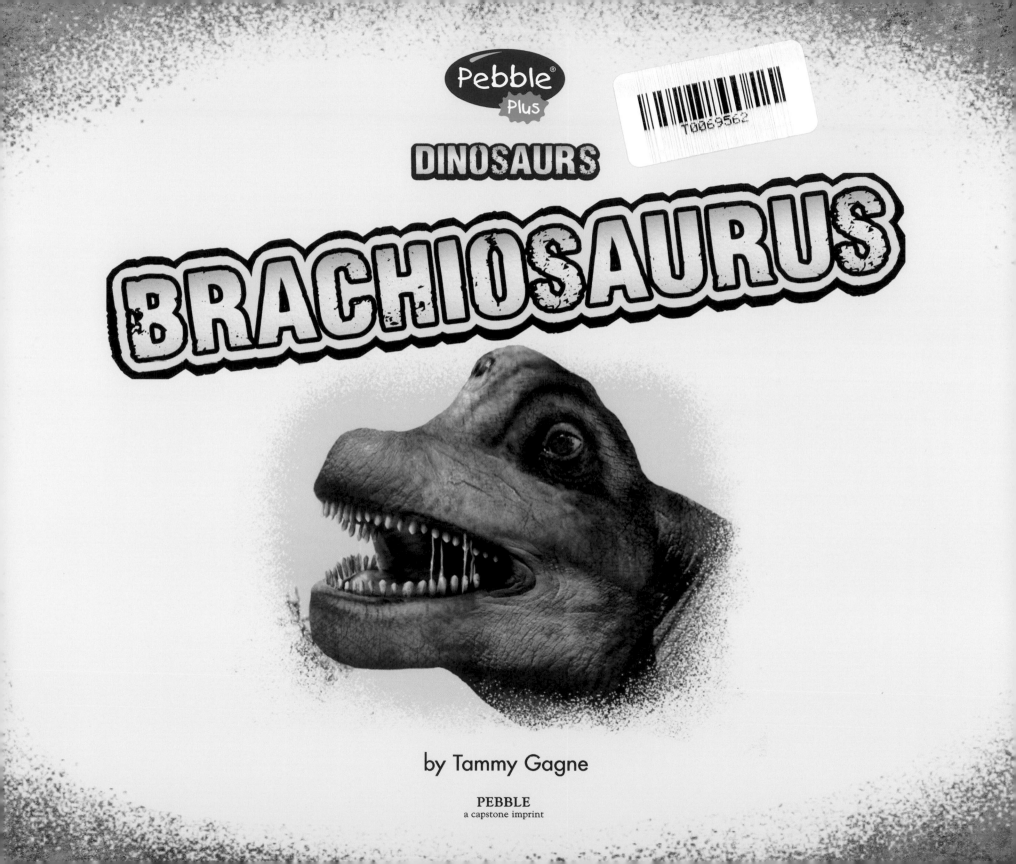

Pebble® Plus

DINOSAURS

BRACHIOSAURUS

by Tammy Gagne

PEBBLE
a capstone imprint

Pebble Plus is published by Pebble,
1710 Roe Crest Drive, North Mankato, Minnesota 56003
www.capstonepub.com

Library of Congress Cataloging-in-Publication Data
Names: Gagne, Tammy, author.
Title: Brachiosaurus / by Tammy Gagne.
Description: North Mankato, Minnesota : an imprint of Pebble, [2019] |
Series: Pebble plus. Dinosaurs | Audience: Age 4–8.
Identifiers: LCCN 2018002967 (print) | LCCN 2018009263 (ebook) |
ISBN 9781515795636 (eBook PDF) | ISBN 9781515795513 (hardcover) |
ISBN 9781515795575 (paperback)
Subjects: LCSH: Brachiosaurus—Juvenile literature.
Classification: LCC QE862.S3 (ebook) | LCC QE862.S3 G3375 2019 (print)
| DDC 567.913—dc23
LC record available at https://lccn.loc.gov/2018002967

Editorial Credits
Hank Musolf, editor; Charmaine Whitman, designer;
Kelly Garvin, media researcher; Laura Manthe, production specialist;
Illustrator, Capstone Press/Jon Hughes

Design Elements
Shutterstock/Krasovski Dmitri

Note to Parents and Teachers

The Dinosaurs set supports national science standards related to life science. This book describes and illustrates brachiosaurus. The images support early readers in understanding the text. The repetition of words and phrases helps early readers learn new words. This book also introduces early readers to subject-specific vocabulary words, which are defined in the Glossary section. Early readers may need assistance to read some words and to use the Table of Contents, Glossary, Read More, Internet Sites, Critical Thinking Questions, and Index sections of the book.

Table of Contents

Meet the Brachiosaurus

Brachiosaurus did not look like the other dinosaurs of its time. This dinosaur's front legs were longer than its back legs. Its long neck made it look a bit like a giraffe.

Brachiosaurus was about twice as tall as a giraffe. This dinosaur stood more than 40 feet (12 meters) tall. Brachiosaurus weighed more than 28 tons (25 metric tons).

Lots of Leaves

Brachiosaurus was an herbivore. This means it survived by eating plants. It could reach leaves on top of the biggest trees.

Brachiosaurus had teeth shaped like spoons. It used them to strip the leaves from tree branches. But the dinosaur swallowed its food whole.

Scientists think brachiosaurus spent most of its time feeding. It needed to eat 880 pounds (400 kilograms) of plants each day.

Living Long Ago

Brachiosaurus lived in Africa, Europe, and North America. Its bones have been found in all of these places. They date back to 150 million years ago.

This dinosaur likely stayed on flat land. Brachiosaurus could feed off many trees without moving its feet. It just moved its neck.

Safety in Size and Numbers

Brachiosaurus traveled in herds.

These groups stayed in one

place as long as they had food.

Then they would move

to a new area.

Scientists do not think adult brachiosaurus had any predators. Older brachiosaurus protected younger ones if a bigger dinosaur came near.

Glossary

herbivore—an animal that only eats plants

herd—a large group of animals that lives or moves together

predator—an animal that hunts other animals for food

scientist—a person who studies the way the world works

Read More

Arlon, Penelope and Tory Gordon-Harris. *Dino Safari: A LEGO Adventure in the Real World.* New York: Scholastic, 2016.

Hughes, Catherine D. *First Big Book of Dinosaurs.* Washington, D.C.: National Geographic, 2011.

Nunn, Daniel. *Brachiosaurus.* Chicago: Heinemann Library, 2015.

Rissman, Rebecca. *Brachiosaurus and Other Long-Necked Dinosaurs: The Need-to-Know Facts.* Mankato, Minn.: Capstone Press, 2016.

Critical Thinking Questions

1. Why do you think brachiosaurus spent so much of its time eating?

2. How do scientists know how big brachiosaurus was?

3. Why do you think the size of brachiosaurus kept predators from hunting it?

Index